A QUESTION OF COPYRIGHT

SECOND EDITION

ERIC A.THORN

Jay books

Jay books
30 The Boundary, Langton Green, Tunbridge Wells, Kent TN3 0YB

Other titles by Eric A. Thorn include:

Understanding Copyright: A Practical Guide (Jay books)
Let's Sing and Make Music (Jay books)
Project the Right Image (Jay books)
The Chosen Few (with Roger Jones) (Christian Music Ministries)
Tell me the stories of Jesus (with Roger Jones) (McCrimmon)

First edition   1983, published by Third Day Enterprises
Re-issued   1985 by Jay books
Second edition 1989

© 1983, 1989 Eric A. Thorn

All rights reserved. No part of this publication may be reproduced or transmitted in any form or by any means, electronic or mechanical, including photocopying, recording, or any information storage and retrieval system, without permission in writing from the publishers.

This book is sold subject to the Standard Conditions of Sale of Net Books and may not be resold in the UK below the net price given by the publishers in their current price list.

ISBN: 1 870404 05 X

Typeset by Solo Typesetting, Maidstone
Printed by Gospel Communication, Tunbridge Wells

PREFACE TO THE SECOND EDITION

With the rapid development of futuristic technology, especially within the information and desktop publishing sector, the Church has realized that it needs to be in the forefront. But with every purchase of contemporary hardware comes a sheet or two of small print. For those who manage to wade through to the bottom line there's usually some comment or other about copyright.

Copyright legislation is far from easy to interpret! So, a few years ago, Eric A. Thorn helped many churches and schools when he brought out the first edition of *A Question of Copyright*, a compilation of the most common questions put to him as a copyright adviser.

The first edition of *A Question of Copyright* ran into several printings. During its five-year life the author was asked new, additional questions, especially at seminars and other events where he was speaking. Such questions, together with the passage of the *Copyright, Designs and Patents Act 1988*, proved the need for a completely new edition. This is it!

The author has been heavily involved in the printing and publishing industries for many years, and is a member of the Publishers Association Copyright Committee. A committed Christian, his writing activities include other practical booklets, hymns and songs, book reviews and editorial work. He will happily answer questions on copyright sent to the publishers, provided a stamped, addressed envelope is enclosed.

This booklet is not a translation of the laws but seeks to impart a better understanding of them. Every care has been taken to ensure that the information given is correct. However, the publishers point out that the text is based on the author's personal interpretation of the copyright laws. Neither the publisher nor the author can accept responsibility for any errors in, or omissions from, the text.

GENERAL INTRODUCTION TO COPYRIGHT

I always thought that anything with the word 'copyright' on it could be copied willy-nilly! Am I right?

Sorry — no! I have to admit that *copyright* does sound rather misleading. But the word actually tells you that someone, somewhere, owns the exclusive right to copy the work on which that word appears! Nobody else may copy it, willy-nilly or otherwise, without the prior consent of that person.

What is 'copyright' exactly?

Good question! By pure definition, *copyright* means *having the right to copy*. Once an idea has been translated into either a tangible or a retrievable format, then the owner of that format has the sole right to copy it in any way they wish, and also has the right to grant other persons the right to copy it. A *tangible* format is when, for example, a song or hymn has been written down onto paper, or recorded onto a tape, or a photograph has been taken. A *retrievable* format is when, again for example, a program is electronically encoded into a computer for retrieving at a later date, either on a visual display screen or as a hard copy.

Who, then, is the 'copyright owner' of a particular work?

The person who owns the tangible form of their original work, or the basis of a retrievable format of it, such as a computer disk or tape.

Are you suggesting that 'copyright works' are items of property?

Yes — intellectual property! If you own a television, that television is your personal property. In a similar way, if you own the copyright of a particular work, then that work is your very own personal property.

In that case, may I sell my copyright to a publisher?

Indeed you may. The usual term for such a sale is *assignment*. In other words, you would assign your copyright to the publisher.

Should you sell (or even give away) your copyright, the arrangement must be agreed by exchange of letters or other form of contract. But remember that once you have given up your copyright, *you* will need permission should you wish to make copies of your own work!

How is copyright protected in law?

Through Acts of Parliament. The *Copyright, Designs and Patents Act, 1988* came into force in 1989.

Copyright law is extremely complicated, and sometimes items of copyright legislation appear to be loose-ended and open to interpretation in a variety of ways. However, the fact is that the law does endeavour to protect all forms of property ownership from theft and abuse, including that of copyright.

Would you kindly elucidate this business of copyright ownership being like property ownership?

I'll try! A piece of writing belongs to the author, music belongs to the composer, a photograph belongs to the photographer — in exactly the same way as your clothes, car, television, etc., belong to you. A car-thief is known as such because he takes a car belonging to somebody else. Someone who evades the copyright law by copying something without permission is just as guilty of theft.

A baker produces bread which he sells for his livelihood. Writers and composers produce words and/or music which they sell in order to make a living. To reproduce something, in any way, without prior permission, invariably means that the copyright owner is being deprived of income.

When does copyright come into operation, and how long does it last?

Copyright exists from the moment an idea has been put into a tangible or retrievable form. For example, if you have written a song, you are the owner of the copyright in that song once you have written it down or recorded it onto tape.

For words and music, photographs, etc., the copyright subsists until 50 years (70 years in the Federal Republic of Germany) after the death of the author/composer. This applies even if the author/composer has assigned their copyright to another party, including a publishing company.

Items such as sound recordings and cinematograph films are granted a copyright term of 50 years from the date of first being made available to the public.

My friend has composed a tune for my poem. If she dies before me, does her copyright last until 50 years after my death?

No. Her copyright will expire 50 years after her death, which means that, in your example, anyone could then use her tune but would still need permission to use your words at that time.

If I die, who grants permission to use my work during the 50 years immediately following my death?

Whoever you have left your copyright to in your will. If you die without making a will, copyright ownership usually passes automatically to the next of kin.

It so happens I've composed some tunes myself. What's the procedure if somebody else wants to produce some arrangements of my music?

Section 21 of the *Copyright, Designs and Patents Act, 1988* declares that making an arrangement or transcription of a musical work is an act restricted by the copyright in that work. In other words, assuming that you own the copyright in the original music, somebody wishing to produce an arrangement must obtain your permission to do so.

© and ℗ SYMBOLS

On published works a letter 'C' often appears enclosed by a circle. What does this mean, and when should it be used?

This is the symbol displayed on copyright works in countries that are signatories to the *Universal Copyright Convention.* It is intended to indicate that any work on which it appears is in copyright and therefore must not be reproduced without permission. It should appear on any copyright work that is likely to be sent abroad, although it is preferable to use it on any copyright work whether the work is likely to reach foreign shores or not. The symbol is normally followed by the date or year when the work came into existence, and/or the name of the copyright owner.

Is the international copyright symbol obligatory?

No, since in law the onus is on somebody wishing to copy a work to check whether or not the work is in copyright and, if so, to obtain the necessary permission. The symbol is designed to help copyright owners to make it clear that their works are in copyright.

I have noticed that the copyright symbol sometimes appears against a company name. Why should this be?

Usually, the author/composer has assigned their copyright to that company. Alternatively, under the terms of specific contracts, the author/composer may have contracted the rights for a particular *edition* to the publishers. In this latter case, it is normal practice for the phrase 'copyright in this edition' to appear next to the copyright symbol and before the company name.

I've noticed on various records and tapes that, in addition to the copyright symbol, there is often a letter 'P' in a circle. Is this something to do with copyright?

Yes. In view of the fact that copyright in sound recordings runs out after 50 years from the date they were first made available to the public, this symbol stands for *year of first publication* (the 'P' stands for 'published'). The symbol is always followed by the year of original publication, so that by adding 50 to that year you can establish the year in which the *copyright in the recording* will expire.

You are implying that there could be more than one copyright in a recording. Please clarify!

The copyright which lasts 50 years from original release date is the *mechanical-copyright*. This is owned by the person who made or commissioned the actual *recording*, usually the record publisher.

Secondly, there is the copyright of the *work recorded*, which is owned by the author/composer (or anyone to whom they have assigned it) and expires 50 years after their deaths.

There could also be somebody else who owns the copyright in the *arrangement* of the work recorded.

Confused? — No, well done!

There's a 'P' in a circle on the labels of some of my clothes. Does this mean that there is a copyright in clothing?

There is copyright in clothing design, patterns, and so on. But the symbol you are referring to is an international garment symbol. It is printed on the labels of garments that are dry cleanable. Sometimes the symbol is printed with 'X' over the top of the 'P'. This means that the garment is not dry cleanable.

I WRITE THE SONGS — PROVING COPYRIGHT OWNERSHIP

I'm the bass guitarist in a group made up of members of a youth club. The vocalist and I often write our own songs and we are trying to raise the cash to release a recording to sell at gigs. We've been told that if the 'P' symbol and the year of first publication of the recording aren't printed on the label, or whatever, our recording is not subject to copyright protection. Is this the case, because we're worried that other people might legally be able to copy our recording without needing permission and without paying us anything for the privilege.

I'm surprised that anyone should have told you that, and whoever it was must have been misinformed — or, possibly, you have misunderstood what was being advised. The law is quite clear that you and your friend own the copyright in your songs. If you record them, or pay a studio to record them for you, then you will also own the copyright in that recording.

Your concern about the possibility of other people taping your record is shared by everybody who is involved in the recording industry around the world! It is because of this concern that you are strongly advised to incorporate the 'P' symbol and year of release either on your record sleeve or label, or both. You are then reminding others that the recording is in copyright for 50 years from the publication year.

Some of the youth club members have duplicated copies of the words of some of our songs. How can I prove that I own the copyright (as I generally write the words) should a copy fall into the 'wrong' hands?

Proving copyright ownership can sometimes be extremely difficult, especially as there is no organized system of registering copyright like, for example, the registration of a trade mark or the patent in an invention.

The best thing to do, it is generally believed, is to post a copy of the item(s) you have written by registered mail to *yourself*. Identify the envelope in some way so that you are aware of the contents, and retain the packet (after it has been delivered to you) *unopened* until it is required to prove copyright ownership, e.g. in a court of law. In court, the postmark will prove that the work was *in existence* upon the *date of posting*.

Once the post office has delivered the registered envelope to you it is, of course, absolutely essential that you keep it in a safe place. Many people deposit such items with their bank.

Registered post is expensive. Is there any cheaper method?

If you're not over-bothered about the possibility of having to prove ownership of a given work, you could send it to yourself by Recorded Delivery. However, this is not recommended because it is believed that registered post is more likely to be considered favourably in Court. Bear in mind that, again, the postmark will prove that the work was *in existence* upon the date of posting.

In terms of value, presumably you would prefer to pay the little extra for the benefit of the upmarket service!

I heard that there was some office where you had to pay a fee and register your copyright. Is this not the case?

Under the *Copyright, Designs and Patents Act, 1988* no formal registration is required. Probably, you've heard of the Stationers' Hall Copyright Registry, Ludgate Hill, London, EC4M 7DD. There used to be a legal requirement to register copyright works with them, but this requirement ceased in 1923. However, they still maintain a register, presumably as a commercial service, but this, again, serves only to prove the *existence* of a work upon the *date of registration*.

Any other suggestions for proving copyright ownership?

Another method is to take a copy of your work to a Commissioner for Oaths and swear that it is your own original work. This would call for the payment of the professional fees ruling at the time. In practice, this again would only prove the *existence* of your work upon a *given date*.

You keep on emphasising the proof of 'existence' rather than 'ownership' and I reckon you are trying to evade my question. Please give a straight answer!

The situation is quite straight-forward: you cannot prove actual ownership. You can only prove that a work was *in existence* in a *material form* upon a *given date*. In the case of a dispute, the Court would have to make the final decision.

If at all possible, no work of any description should be allowed an airing to anyone prior to taking one of the precautions suggested above.

PHOTOCOPYING

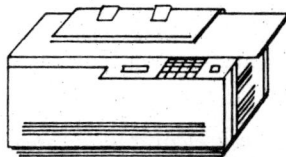

Let me get this quite clear about my song (or, for that matter, anything else that I may own the copyright of). Are you suggesting that nobody may use it for any purpose without my permission?

That's right, so long as you don't assign your copyright to any other party. But there's always the exception to every rule. In this case, the exception is photocopying.

But that's just what I don't want people to do!

Have patience, please! Photocopying of certain material is permitted by the 1988 Act of Parliament for purposes of *fair dealing*. This includes copying of items for research, private study, judicial proceedings, and so on. In these respects, it is wise to assume that only one copy of any item may be made. Multiple copying without specific permission is always illegal.

So what exactly is 'fair dealing'?

Fair dealing is *generally accepted* as meaning, in the case of a book or article, one extract up to 4 000 words *or* a series of extracts, each extract having a maximum of 3 000 words, and the total of the series of extracts amounting to not more that 8 000 words. However, in any instance of copying, the actual maximum permitted is a total of 10% of the work being copied.

In the case of such items as poems, essays, short works and music, permission is always required.

I belong to my church's amateur dramatic society. We wanted to photocopy a play that went out of copyright some years ago, but the publishers said we couldn't do this unless we typed it all out first. Why should this be?

Because typesetting is the copyright of the publisher of any given work. This typesetting copyright subsists for a period of 25 years from the date of printing. So, although you may have the right to reproduce something, in this case a play, it is always possible that you will have to copy it by hand unless you first obtain the publisher's permission to photocopy his typography!

It's rumoured that teachers sometimes make class sets of copyright material. Do special dispensations apply to teachers?

There are *no* special dispensations for teachers, but — subject to stringent conditions — class sets of certain material may be photocopied by teachers whose schools have taken out a licence with the *Copyright Licensing Agency*, 33 Alfred Place, London, WC1E 7DP. Sometimes 'blanket' licences are taken out by local education authorities, to cover all of the schools, colleges, and other educational institutions within their control. Incidentally, the CLA licence scheme is not restricted to educational bodies; anybody with a reprographic machine may obtain a CLA licence.

Does the CLA licence cover all manner of photocopying?

No. The scheme was originally set up by the professional associations which represent literary copyright owners, with the objective of creating a fair balance between the requirements of both the copyright owners and the users of their materials. So, at present anyway, only *literary* works published in books or journals are covered. Certain publications are excluded from the scheme, probably for contractual reasons, but full details are available direct from the Copyright Licensing Agency.

Could I photocopy an entire book under the CLA Scheme?

This would not be possible because the actual proportion of a work which may be reproduced is limited. As you will appreciate, such limitations act as safety valves to ensure that copying is kept to a sensible level. In any case, it would surely be cheaper for you to purchase another copy of a book!

It's good to note that there is help for teachers using literary copyright materials, but is there any scheme that would benefit me, as a teacher of music?

There is a licensing agreement in respect of the *extra-curricular* use of copyright music in schools. This agreement is between the Performing Right Society and the various local education authorities in England, Scotland and Wales. However, the scheme covers only state and voluntary aided schools in these countries, and is subject to review from time to time. I suggest you contact your local education authority, in order to check whether or not your requirements are covered.

ROYALTIES

You've hinted that writers receive payments when their works are copied. Is this how writers earn their living?

Full-time writers and composers depend entirely upon their receipts, though many writers and composers also undertake some other work as well. In the case of published works, copyright owners receive *royalties* on all copies of their work(s) sold. They may also receive payments when their work is used in other ways, for example when items are photocopied for use at a seminar or conference. Sometimes, permission to copy a work is given quite freely, but even in these cases an acknowledgement should be given (e.g. *'Copyright 1989 A.T. Ennyseed, used by kind permission').* So it will be seen that if you reproduce something without permission, you could be robbing someone of part of their earnings.

I've written a Christian song. Peartree Publications have offered to publish it, and pay me a royalty on copies sold. Do you think it is right for me to use a gift of God for financial gain?

I cannot say what is right for you personally, but the fact is that unless you assign your copyright to another party, you are *entitled* to royalties against copies published and sold commercially. You could, however, request that such royalties be donated to a charitable body.

Sometimes a Christian, having written a hymn or song, may feel that it belongs to the Lord. He or she takes no interest in copyright or royalties as these appear to be concerned only with selfish motives. There is nothing wrong in feeling this way, but it is important to recognize that in the blessing of inspiration for a song, God has also entrusted a gift which requires wise stewardship.

Yes, but I would not feel right about accepting money for the use of the song in worship/ evangelism.

Publication is really a joint effort between writer and publisher. It involves sharing in every sense. Any financial returns, having been properly shared with the publisher on an agreed basis, may be used according to individual conscience and perhaps to greater effect than the song itself. You could, for example, prayerfully consider giving any income generated from your song to a missionary society or evangelistic organization.

Do try to avoid the extreme attitude of total disinterest in the financial aspects of publication.

What you say does seem to make sense now I think about it. By the way, what about those publishers who ask you to pay them to publish songs or books?

The fact is that reputable publishers do *not* ask you to pay them to publish your work. They take all publication risks, and pay you in accordance with the contract you have made with them. I have noticed that some of the so-called *vanity publishers* advertise in the classified columns of the religious press. Be advised to steer clear of anyone who offers you publication of your work in return for a fee.

The exception to this rule is in connection with specialized, highly technical books with a limited readership potential. In special circumstances, these may be jointly financed by the author and the publisher.

COPYING HYMNS — PRODUCING A PERSONAL SONGBOOK

We sometimes photocopy the words of very old hymns which we know are out of copyright. Presumably, based on what you've been saying, this is quite legal?

If you're photocopying them from a book that has been published within the past 25 years, then you do need permission from the publisher. This is because of the 25 year copyright on typesetting.

A *printing history* is normally given on the reverse of the title page of most hymn and song books. Check this prior to contacting the publisher. It may save you a stamp!

My church is planning to produce a fellowship song book. Is this OK? The real problem is, nobody seems to know how to contact the various copyright owners in order to get their permission. Any thoughts on this one?

I assume that your anthology will be collected from a number of hymn and song books. Check in the full music editions of each of the books you are taking items from, as most music editions give a list of the relevant copyright owners or agents. Some editions may tell you if items are *public domain* which means they are out of copyright and no permission to reproduce them is necessary.

When the music editions do not give you the information you require, you should write to the publishers of these editions. In many cases you will discover that the publishers are acting on behalf of the author/composer. If not, they will either forward your request, or inform you of the address to which you should write.

When writing to a publisher or copyright owner, please remember the courtesy of enclosing a stamped, addressed envelope.

Should you be utilizing a substantial number of more recently published hymns and songs, you may find it beneficial to take out a licence with the *Christian Music Association*, Glyndley Manor, Stone Cross, Pevensey, East Sussex, BN24 5BS.

Does the CMA licence authorize 'carte blanche' copying?

Negative! All forms of copying must be kept to reasonable levels, and current details of the CMA restrictions are available direct from the Christian Music Association at the address I've just given you. As with the CLA scheme which I mentioned earlier, the CMA licence does *not* cover everything. You are advised to check exactly which publishers and publications are currently included. Certain individual items within songbooks may not necessarily be covered, for example.

I'm sorry, I failed to make it clear that the songs we are collecting do not appear to be in any hymn books! . . . So what can we do?

Telephone MCPS on 01-769-4400 during normal office hours, and ask to speak to the Index Section. They have an index containing copyright information on 1½ million songs.

Alternatively, contact the Christian Music Association, telephone number Eastbourne (0323) 440440, to enquire whether or not they can help.

I attend a community church and we're actually in the process of writing round to publishers, seeking permission to use various items in a loose-leaf book we're preparing for our own use. Some copyright owners have indicated that they will charge us for the use of their material. Should we pay?

If you ignore a request for payment, you may rest assured that the next communication you receive will not be so polite. The eventual result will almost certainly be your church being taken to Court and having to find a considerably higher amount than that originally required.

If you decide not to use their material, it would be courteous to write and thank them for their trouble, explaining that a decision has been reached and that their work will not now be included. If you have received an invoice, return it with such a letter as you will not be expected to pay for anything you have not used.

Once a month we have a 'Family Service' at my church. For this, the vicar always duplicates the hymns onto a sheet. These hymn sheets are thrown away after use. Should the vicar have permission to duplicate for this purpose?

The fact is that *any* form of reproduction, without authority, is illegal.

You will be pleased to know, however, that for reproducing the words of hymns in a temporary format for use in a worship service there is often no charge imposed. But most copyright owners will insist on a credit, e.g. *'Copyright 1989 I. Rytem, used by kind permission'*.

Do not expect copyright owners to be so generous if they discover unlicenced use of their works — unless you can *prove* that you have taken all reasonable steps to obtain permission and/or trace the owner of the copyright in any particular instance.

But the vicar has said quite categorically that you don't need permission to duplicate the words from the book we use, which is 'Living Lord'.

He's quite right! Certain recently-published hymn and song books have included a *copyright note* giving automatic permission for groups who have purchased a copy of the book to reproduce the words of individual items, in a temporary format, subject to the usual credit appearing.

Such collections include *Living Lord* (Josef Weinberger). The publishers are to be commended for their initiative

I trust that your vicar is including the appropriate credits on your monthly service sheets.

What about running off a few copies of four-part songs for the church choir?

As stringent rules apply to the copying of music, the rule of thumb is to obtain written permission to reproduce music. And this applies even if you require only a few copies for your choir or musical group.

An event we are planning would be seriously handicapped if a particular piece of music was not used. We have not written for permission for fear that permission might be refused, or it might cost too much. The copyright owner will be no worse off for our using his music, but the Lord's work would be harmed if we don't.

Personally, I've not heard of any copyright owner refusing permission for their work to be used. After all, composers and authors are particularly keen to see their work used as widely as possible. My experience is that most copyright owners give permission either at no charge or at a nominal charge for non-commercial purposes. I feel that you should apply for permission straight away in view of the fact that the Lord's work is more likely to be harmed if the copyright owner discovered the illegal use of his material.

OVERHEAD PROJECTOR

At my church we have someone who writes the words of choruses, etc. on to overhead projector transparencies, so that what we're singing is projected onto a screen. The guy who does all this says it's all right, especially as he can easily throw the ohp transparencies out at short notice. What do you think?

I think that he is admitting he is in the wrong when he says he can easily dispose of the transparencies! Technically, I wonder if those of you who allow this practice are aiding and abetting? The fact is that one such transparency is equal to giving one duplicated copy to each person in the congregation. So, the rule is to get permission and see that the transparency includes an acknowledgement.

You may be interested to know that professionally produced overhead projector transparencies, slides and wallcharts of most popular hymns and carols are available from Scaids, 51 York Place, Edinburgh, EH1 3JE (write for their current catalogue).

I have seen lots of ohp transparencies labelled 'Songs of Fellowship'. Is there any restriction on their use?

The 'Songs of Fellowship' ohp transparencies are published by Kingsway, who say that their transparencies are sold as a sensible alternative to the printed words editions. Kingsway inform me that they hope the transparencies are used only by those churches and other organizations that have purchased them for their own use. They should not be copied, for example!

RECORDS/TAPES

At my school, a record or tape is often used as part of the morning assembly. Is this legally acceptable?

Yes! Copyright legislation within the United Kingdom declares that copyright is not infringed if a sound recording is caused to be heard in public as part of the activities of any organization not conducted for profit and whose objectives are concerned with the advancement of religion, education or social welfare.

What about using, say, a musicassette for other purposes, or even re-recording an item from a record?

Such recordings will often or invariably include music, and if the initials *MCPS* appear on the cassette or record labels, then the *Mechanical-Copyright Protection Society*, 41 Streatham High Road, London, SW16 1ER, are the agents for the music publisher. They will issue licences and collect fees in respect of the published music on his behalf. There are other agencies, incidentally, but MCPS is probably the biggest and most well-known.

The MCPS (or other agency) licence grants permission to record the music in question or re-record from the already published recording.

And this licence also gives you permission to play the recording in public?

No! Licences for this purpose are issued by the *Performing Right Society*, 29/33 Berners Street, London, W1P 4AA.

PRS also issues licences for the live performance of copyright music, so it might be worthwhile to drop them a line if you organize gospel concerts and the like. As with MCPS, the PRS acts only on behalf of its own members. It is the responsibility of the organizer of an event to apply for the necessary licences from PRS.

Is there any set-up which acts on behalf of the record companies?

Yes. *Phonographic Performance Ltd*, 14 Ganton Street, London, W1V 1LB acts for record companies in much the same way as PRS acts for writers and composers. If using a commercial recording, therefore, permission must often also be obtained from PPL.

Does this mean I don't need to get any special permission from record publishers?

Although it's additional work on your part, it's as well to advise the publishers of commercial recordings if you plan to use any of their wares, in any way. Some record publishing houses may insist on giving their individual permission, even though a licence has been obtained from PPL.

The record company makes no charge for this additional permission, PPL being their appointed collector of royalties. It's just that they like to know how their productions are being used.

'LIVE' MUSIC

You mentioned that the Performing Right Society issues licences for the live performance of copyright music. Does this mean that every church should have a PRS licence in respect of hymns and other music used in worship?

No. The Performing Right Society does not charge fees in respect of the *performance* of music at any divine service at any place of worship.

You say 'divine service'. What about music performed at other church, or youth club, events?

For all events other than normal services of worship, you should obtain a licence from the Performing Right Society to cover any music that may be performed 'live'.

LEGAL ACTION

What do you reckon could happen if we simply ignore the copyright laws and, say, have a hymn or song book run off at our local quick print shop?

You might just get away with it, but you could find yourselves at the centre of a long, drawn-out Court case. A four or five figure fine and/or considerable damages and costs (not forgetting your own costs) would be the inevitable result.

If your offence came to light, you would also be obliged to hand over whatever-it-was that proved you were infringing copyright in some way.

In any event, what you are proposing is wrong and you would not expect me to condone such action, surely? Could you carry it out with a clear conscience?

Is there any time limit for bringing action against copyright offenders?

Yes. A summons in respect of infringement of copyright may be lodged at any time up till six years from the alleged date of infringement.

Aren't such cases normally settled out of Court?

It is believed that many cases of copyright infringement are, indeed, settled out of Court. However, evasion of the copyright laws is now being taken more and more seriously, and action for compensation from infringers is being pursued with continually renewed vigour.

A few years ago there was a lot of talk about some school being 'done', but you don't hear much about copyright cases. Does someone get sued every-so-often to frighten everyone into being 'good' for a bit?

The school in question was Oakham School, Leicestershire. In 1981 they were ordered to pay £4 250 including £400 exemplary damages (plus their own costs). A year earlier, the Wolverhampton Education Authority were ordered to pay £1 300 damages, plus costs of over £2 000 (and their own costs). Both defendants were taken to Court by the Music Publishers' Association, who are one of the many professional bodies pressing for the heaviest penalties when infringement of copyright is proven in Court.

I don't really believe that a case comes up in Court now and then just to frighten people. It's just that many cases are settled out of Court, and only the local papers are likely to mention minor cases.

Nobody would really take a church to Court though, would they?

Well, they would. There have been two such cases, to my knowledge, in recent years. And any church that is breaking the law is not a good Christian witness by a long chalk!

Is it possible to take legal action against infringers in another country?

Of course it is! In the same year that Oakham School were defending themselves in the English Court, some British publishers were occupied with a college in Virginia, USA.
Oxford University Press, Theodore Presser Co. and Novello & Co. Ltd jointly agreed on a settlement with the American college. In bringing action, the publishers alleged wilful infringement of copyright, and stated that copyrights owned by them were violated by being photocopied without permission. The defendants agreed to pay damages and attorneys' fees, and to refrain from any further such photocopying.

Is it wrong to use a song sheet that you suspect has been produced without reference to the copyright owners of the songs?

Oh yes. It is against the law to *knowingly* have and/or use infringing copies of anything.
Stiffer penalties are now being imposed upon offenders found guilty of knowingly having or using infringing copies. It is to be hoped that such penalties will have the desired effect.

CHRISTIAN WITNESS

I'm on the Christian Fellowship committee at the college where I'm a student. We photocopy our own chorus sheets, and also copy items into our CF magazine. Presumably, this is the sort of thing which copyright owners would turn a blind eye to? After all, we are only using Christian material for Christian purposes!

The best advice I can offer you is to destroy your chorus sheets, and start afresh! If you find it helpful to duplicate the items you wish to use, I cannot too strongly impress upon you the importance of obtaining permission from the relevant copyright owners! With reference to your magazine, again, you *must* obtain permission before reproducing *any* copyright item, whatever it is.

You're joking! I'm only talking about private use in the college Christian Fellowship!

I'm *not* joking. No matter what the circumstances, Christians are *not* above the law (as some might have us believe). We are required to abide by the laws of those set in authority over us: see *Romans 13, verses 1 and 2.*

But they are only duplicated items, and we don't sell our magazines!

No buts! The law is the law, and there are no exceptions, not even for Christians. Let me ask you a question: Is the Lord truly glorified by all those duplicated hymn and chorus sheets, overhead projector transparencies, and items reproduced in newsletters and church magazines, without prior licence? Or, if permission has been obtained, without the customary acknowledgement included?

I see what you mean. Not only are we breaking the law, we are offending God and hindering our Christian witness.

I'm afraid so. I think your fellowship and witness will be strengthened considerably once you've thrown out your song sheets! I suggest your next bible study be based on Romans 13!

INFORMING THE PUBLIC

You have, quite rightly, implied that ignorance of the law is no excuse for breaking it. Is anything being done to educate people such as myself, an ordinary member of the public, about what I am allowed, or not allowed, to copy?

I accept that the inherent problem facing the public is that, very often, it is assumed that published material may be copied without permission. In certain instances it is possible to make one copy of a brief extract of a work.

Certainly, in order to try and pave the way towards a better understanding of the law, organizations such as the *Periodical Publishers Association* make regular announcements in the media, warning everybody to think before making any copy of anything.

Commercial publishers have also tried to help. Jay books, for example, — please pardon the commercial! — have published my own book on the subject, entitled *Understanding Copyright: A Practical Guide*. This deals in more detail than is possible here with all aspects of copyright.

VIDEO AND FILMING IN CHURCH

I'm getting married soon and a friend of mine has offered to make a videotape of the wedding ceremony. I mentioned this to the vicar when my fiancé and I went to see him, but he said he can't allow it to be done, and mumbled something about copyright. Can he put his foot down like this?

I'm afraid so. Permission for videotaping and/or filming in or around church premises needs to be obtained in advance from the incumbent, priest, or minister. Not only this, but strictly speaking, unless the tape is intended for your own private use at home, you also require the permission of *every* participant in the service.

I'm an Anglican, and my clergyman recently said something about the Church of England being concerned about getting mixed up in the video piracy debate, and he was referring to videotaping weddings. What's he on about?

You will appreciate that I can't answer on behalf of your clergyman! But, apparently, Church House does receive enquiries from incumbents around the country, and endeavours to explain the copyright implications. In February 1983, the *Daily Mail* reported that some members of the clergy in the Warrington area had decided to ban videotaping of weddings at their respective churches. This action was taken because the clergy in question were worried lest the law should be broken, however unintentionally.

In view of the fact that the Performing Right Society doesn't charge for the live performance of music in worship, may we assume that no permission is required for recording or videotaping music in church?

No 'get-out' for that one, I'm afraid! You do require permission to record any copyright music. Incidentally, do remember that older pieces may well have recent arrangements and therefore be protected by copyright.

As the Mechanical-Copyright Protection Society are the principal agents for copyright music you may apply direct to them for a licence.

Can I get a licence from MCPS to cover the music which will be recorded on the video of my wedding?

If the copyright owners are members of MCPS (and it's most probable that they will be), then the answer is the affirmative. The MCPS licence covers all their members' works.

It covers the recording of one master tape and up to nine copies. The licence is granted on condition that no copies of the videotape are sold or used for any commercial purpose.

I'd like to start a business making videotapes of weddings. Do I have to obtain an MCPS licence for every commission I get?

Your business would qualify for an annual 'company' licence. You should contact the Video Department at MCPS for full details.

We had our wedding ceremony videotaped. But the organist kept making comments about wanting to be paid under the 'Performers Protection Acts'. Should we have paid him?

The *Performers Protection Acts* were included amongst the various Acts of Parliament that were repealed by the *Copyright, Designs and Patents Act, 1988*. As I understand the legislation, if the tape was for your own private and personal use at home, there was no requirement for you to pay the organist.

The 'Wedding March' did not come out very well on our videotape, so we'd like to dub it on from a record. What's the procedure for this?

Write to the publisher of the record (you should find the address on the record sleeve) explaining the circumstances and requesting the appropriate permission.

At my church, the minister often reads a poem when he conducts weddings. Is it OK for him to do this at a ceremony which is being recorded?

If the poem is copyright, it may be used only if the copyright owner has granted their permission.

And if permission is not forthcoming?

Then the poem (or, for that matter, any other literary work) may not legally be used.

At my place of worship, we sometimes videotape special services for showing to people, like the housebound. We had to get permission to record an evangelistic song used at our Anniversary services earlier this year. However, the publisher in question stipulated that the tape had to be erased within one year from the date of recording. Do you think this is reasonable?

Any copyright owner may impose any conditions with regard to the use of their property. Failure to comply with such conditions could result in proceedings under the law of contract. Remember, permission to use copyright material is obtained by an exchange of letters which, under English law, constitutes a legal and binding contract. Any conditions must be stipulated in the relevant correspondence.

In this instance, it is my humble opinion that use of the videotape for one year is perfectly reasonable. The people to whom you show your video have probably all seen it within a few weeks from the actual service. And then you will probably need to re-use the tape to record a further service.

We are planning a video tape library. Can we make a hire charge, or should we use a free loan scheme and invite donations?

At the time this book went to press, there was no apparent legal reason against nominal hire charges in respect of a video tape library, though I understand that some local authorities have limiting byelaws, so it would be best to check with your local administration first. However, it could be best simply to invite donations, because Section 66 of the 1988 Act provides that either a rental licensing scheme or royalty payment scheme *may* be introduced at any time.

PRE-RECORDED VIDEOS

At our club for young married couples, one of our members sometimes hires a video film from a local video shop for us to see. It's like going to the cinema for free! But is it above board, so to speak?

No, this is absolutely and decidedly wrong. The hire charge levied at such video libraries covers the hirer only in respect of his or her private viewing, together with their immediate family, at home. The small print on videos, which is usually included on the videogram for all to read, generally states something to the effect that the video is supplied for use only in private homes to which other members of the public are not invited.

OK, but how can we have video films without breaking the law?

Firstly, you should plan your meetings several weeks ahead, so that you may approach the video company, or its agents, in good time to obtain permission. Names and addresses are usually printed on the video label, and your colleague can therefore scribble down the appropriate information when visiting the video shop.

Secondly, a number of commercial enterprises have produced films on video that are available on either free loan or a modest hire charge, for showing to such groups as yours. Companies concerned include Shell and British Gas. Catalogues and/or other information are often available for inspection at the reference desk of public libraries.

My church wants to hire a video for use at a mission from a Christian organization that provides videos and films. They tried to get us to hire the film version instead. Don't you think that's a retrograde step?

Thank you for your question! I have checked with several organizations on their attitude. International Films informed me that their company policy is to produce videos for private and domestic viewing at a person's home address, and films for public presentation (particularly at venues where the film quality would be desirable). CTVC, on the other hand, advised me that their policy is to produce videos for viewing at schools and churches, so there is no problem. But you do need their prior permission if your intention is to charge people for admission.

RECORDING TV PROGRAMMES

I'm thinking of renting a videotape recorder, but I'm a bit worried about the 'small print' which states that recording and playback of material may require consent. What does it mean?

Exactly what it says: recording *and* playback may require consent. If you have a video camera you may, of course, record private items, such as your children playing in the garden, and play such items back as often as you like.

But most people, myself included, would only want to record TV programmes. I get the impression that video recorder manufacturers are trying to sell products that you may not be able to use legally! Is it OK to record TV broadcasts?

Yes, under the 1988 UK legislation, domestic off-air recording of television programmes is quite permissible, provided that such recordings are only played back privately in your own home, and that no charge is levied on anybody watching the programmes. Recordings may not be made, without prior consent, for any kind of commercial purposes.

Many people, it is believed, record television programmes on a time-shift basis. That is to say, they happen to be out, possibly on holiday, when their favourite programme is on the air. So they set up their video recorder, and watch their idols at a later time than the original transmission. The tape is then erased when the exercise is repeated on another occasion.

Is it necessary to get permission from the participants of a TV programme prior to recording it?

If the recording you make is for *your own* private and domestic purposes, you do not need to seek permission from the actual performers.

In all other cases, including the private and domestic purposes of *anyone else*, permission from performers is required.

You must be joking! I recorded the Live Aid concert to show to our youth group. How could I get the permission of all those artistes?

If you had played your recording of the concert to your youth group, without prior permission from the transmitting company responsible for the broadcast, that would have constituted a violation of the 'public performance' rights. However, if you had obtained prior written permission you would probably have been covered in respect of the artistes, as the television production company would be acting on their behalf. But it's as well to confirm this point when in correspondence with a television company, should you be involved with some similar situation in the future.

I'm taking an Open University course, and it would help my studies if I could videotape certain Open University programmes that are broadcast on TV. Do I have to go through a whole lot of red tape to do this legally?

If you use the tapes for your own private study at home, there is no problem as far as I can see, because this would be covered by the legislation applicable to domestic off-air recording (see above).

Licences in respect of any other uses of tapes of OU programmes are available from Open University Enterprises, 12 Cofferidge Close, Milton Keynes, MK11 1BY.

VIDEO PIRACY

There are frequent rumours and media reports about video piracy. Can you please explain what 'video piracy' is?

I will try! In the early part of 1983 it was estimated that £1 000 000 were spent each week by the UK public buying *pirate videos*. This is the term given to illegal videotape copies of films and television programmes being sold on a commercial basis. Such pirate copies are generally considered to be of an inferior quality. They are usually sold at much cheaper prices than the recommended retail prices of authentic items.

This sounds like a lucrative business! What effect is it having on the film industry?

The obvious effect is that of robbing the film companies of potential sales of their authentic videotapes. This, in turn, presumably means that there's less money in the kitty for releasing new video titles.

Is anything being done to terminate this piracy?

It's very doubtful whether or not such piracy will ever be completely eliminated; only time will tell. Meanwhile, some publishers of videos are putting security labels on their tapes in an effort to make piracy difficult.

To ensure that they receive back the video tapes that are actually rented out (and not a pirate copy made by the hirer) many video libraries have their tapes marked with a unique ultraviolet security stamp.

I've no evidence to substantiate it, but I reckon I've been sold a pirate videotape. What should I do?

You can refer the matter to the Trading Standards Department of your local government authority. Alternatively, you may telephone the *Video Trade Association* on 01-464 8833. In either case, your report will be confidentially investigated, and if a video pirate is traced, prosecution will be the inevitable result.

Does the Government support the stamping out of video piracy?

Absolutely; as do the Courts, who are now handing out tougher penalties than ever before.

MICROCOMPUTER PROGRAMS

I've heard rumours that computer programs are not protected by copyright. Why is this?

Rumours of this nature were in vogue some years ago. Legislation in force at the time was drawn up prior to the rapid growth of computer technology. Various copyright amendment acts helped towards solving the problem, but our current legislation is perfectly clear: all such items, business programs, games, or whatever, are all protected by copyright for a period of 50 years.

In that case, is there a movement against software piracy?

Indeed there is, and it is known as FAST (the Federation Against Software Theft). As an example of their vigilance, in 1987 they tracked down TOS International in Torquay dealing in software piracy. The proprietor of TOS received twelve months' imprisonment.

At a Magistrates' Court in Essex, in May 1988, another software pirate was fined £4 400 plus costs.

Do you think micros will ever 'catch on' in churches?

Microcomputers have already attracted the Christian community, and will probably soon be considered standard equipment for church offices. Whether used for office purposes or with games and educational programs, they are subject to various copyright and data protection regulations. Gareth Morgan has looked at the subject in some depth in his book *Church Computing: A Strategy* (Jay books).

COPYRIGHT ORGANISATIONS

Apart from those you've already mentioned, are there any other organizations concerned with copyright matters?

Several organizations exist, each representing different kinds of users and owners of copyright works. Some of the main ones are listed below. A fuller list of names and addresses is given in *Understanding Copyright: A Practical Guide.*

BBC Copyright Department
   Broadcasting House, Portland Place, London W1A 1AA
British Copyright Council
   29 Berners Street, London W1P 4AA
Christian Music Association
   Glyndley Manor, Stone Cross, Pevensey, East Sussex BN24 5BS
Copyright Licensing Agency
   33 Alfred Place, London WC1E 7DP
Independent Television Association
   Knighton House, 56 Mortimer Street, London W1N 8AN
Mechanical-Copyright Protection Society
   Elgar House, 41 Streatham High Road, London SW16 1ER
Music Publishers Association
   Kingsway House, 103 Kingsway, London WC2B 6QX
Performing Right Society
   29-33 Berners Street, London W1P 4AA
Phonographic Performance
   Ganton House, 14 Ganton Street, London W1V 1LB
Publishers Association
   19 Bedford Square, London WC1B 3HJ
Video Copyright Protection Society
   Visnews House, Cumberland Avenue, London NW10 7EH

FURTHER QUESTIONS

If we have other questions, or if we would like to invite you to participate in a seminar or conference, how can we contact you?

Write to me c/o Jay books, 30 The Boundary, Langton Green, Tunbridge Wells, TN3 0YB. Please enclose a stamped, self-addressed envelope, as the cost of postage can be rather high if I should receive several enquiries together!

Understanding Copyright: A Practical Guide

Copyright is one of those peculiar commodities that affect most of us either directly or indirectly. We read newspapers, magazines and books, watch television and video, listen to records and tapes, or use computer programs, all of which have operated under the control of copyright legislation.

The UK legislation has been revised, by the **Copyright, Designs and Patents Act,** to take account of high tech media and modern-day usage of the multitude of resources that boast copyright protection.

How does this affect – a teacher who wants to photocopy a class set of notes from a text book?

– a club secretary who would like the members to see a video?

– a vicar who desires to duplicate a hymn sheet?

– an individual at home who wants to copy a cassette tape of music or a computer game?

– and so on. The list is endless!

How does it affect you, when you feel that you have a genuine need to utilize 'copyright materials'?

Understanding Copyright is aptly subtitled **A Practical Guide.**

The author explores all these points and more. The pages are written in plain English, to help the reader to comprehend what is sometimes regarded as an incomprehensible subject.

Jay books   ISBN: 1 870404 03 3   £4.95 (by post £5.40)

Acorns from Jay Books

These are booklets designed to help you to communicate. Each is written in simple terms by an expert, to enable you to make the best use of available resources.

(1) # PROJECT THE RIGHT IMAGE *Eric A Thorn*
A practical handbook for Christian bookstall organisers. **£1.00**

A practical concise guide for all who run a church bookstall on how to give it a worthy and worthwhile image. The author is an established book agent with years of marketing experience in Christian publishing.   0 9510086 2 5

20 pages

(2) # GET IT TAPED *Angela Almond*   **£1.85**
Recording and using audio cassettes in church.   32 pages

A comprehensive, but simply written, handbook dealing with the choice and installation of recording equipment, making recordings for various applications, organising a tape library, and what to do if something goes wrong or does not work.   0 9510086 3 3

(3) # STARTING IN VIDEO *Kenneth E Acton*   **£1.50**
The costs and resources needed; including a directory of Christian video producers.   28 pages

A vital primer for would-be video film makers, with guidelines on quality of equipment needed, its cost, desirability of hiring or buying, and expertise needed. Included are addresses and phone numbers of Christian producers who may be approached to undertake projects.   0 9510086 4 1

(4) # LET'S SING & MAKE MUSIC *Eric A Thorn*
£1.20
Developing a music ministry.   20 pages

Valuable advice on how any church can enliven its worship and utilise the musical talents of its members through the co-ordinating work of a Director of Music.   0 9510086 6 8

(5) # COMMUNICATE! *Kim Cook*   **£1.60**
A guide to basic PR for Christians.   28 pages

How the principles of good public relations can be applied to communicating our Christian beliefs to the world. The product, market, methods, media and right style are described for organisations and churches.   0 9510086 7 6

Acorns from Jay Books

In addition to this basic series, we also publish books that give fuller and more detailed information on sound recording, using video, church computing, copyright laws, etc.

(6) **FIRST IMPRESSIONS** *Francis Newing*　　　**£1.50**

Printing the church magazine and other literature.　　　32 pages
A printer describes the alternative ways in which literature may be produced for churches and small organisations and explains the benefits and costs of the various options. A directory of services is included.　　0 9510086 8 4

(7) **CHRISTIAN VIDEOS FOR CHILDREN AND YOUNG PEOPLE** *Trevor Payne*　　**£1.60**

For use in home, church, youth club, school.　　　44 pages
A descriptive guide to available videos for those working with children and teenagers. Contents, age suitability, playing time and suppliers are given.　　0 9510086 9 2

(8) **MICROS WITH A MESSAGE** John Fewings

Computers in Christian youth work　　　**£1.85**

For all thinking of using computers in Sunday school or youth group. It assumes no previous expertise, but is full of practical advice. The various types of games and educational programs are described, with their limitations and advantages.　　32 pages
A 50p voucher is included against the purchase of BIBLEchip software.　　1 870404 04 1

(9) **A QUESTION OF COPYRIGHT** (2ED)

Covering the 1988 Act　　　*Eric A Thorn*　　**£1.50**

An authoritative guide to the requirements of copyright in church and allied uses by a member of the PA copyright committee. The first edition was in constant demand. It has now been completely rewritten to take account of the new Copyright Act, and is backed by an advisory service.　28 pages　1 870404 05 X

AUTHORS. If you have any ideas for technical resource books that you think should be included in our list please let us know. We would be particularly interested in hearing from potential authors, who are advised to contact the publisher, Ken Jackson, to discuss their plans at an early stage.

MAILING LIST. Write to us if you would like your name to be added to our mailing list to receive information on new titles.

BIBLE BACKGROUND GUIDES
FOR TEACHERS AND PUPILS

Drawings for enlargement, illustration, colouring or copying, of people and objects from the land where Jesus lived.

Set 1: People, sheep and shepherds, farming, fishing, bread-making, olives, houses, worship, miscellaneous. *0-7197-0315-8*

Set 2: More people, vines and vineyards, musical instruments, officials, trades, fruit & vegetables, Jerusalem, crib figures, miscellaneous. *0-7197-0316-6*

Set 3: Bible maps and plans.

The ancient Near East (Abraham); The Exodus (Moses); The Two Kingdoms; Palestine in the time of Christ; Eastern Mediterranean in the time of Paul; Jerusalem in New Testament times; Herod's Temple. *0-7197-0347-6*

Other resources available from the National Christian Education Council include the popular "Bright Ideas" series, many titles of which incorporate an excellent section of photocopiable material.

Send for complete list

National Christian Education Council
Robert Denholm House, Nutfield, Redhill, Surrey RH1 4HW
Telephone Nutfield Ridge (0737) 822411. Fax (0737) 822116